GETTING MORE FROM YOUR INVESTMENT IN TRAINING:

# THE 5As FRAMEWORK

STEPHEN J. GILL & SEAN P. MURRAY

GETTING MORE FROM YOUR INVESTMENT IN TRAINING: THE 5AS FRAMEWORK

GETTING MORE FROM YOUR INVESTMENT IN TRAINING:

# THE 5As FRAMEWORK

STEPHEN J. GILL & SEAN P. MURRAY

REALTIME PERFORMANCE
603 STEWART STREET, SUITE 500
SEATTLE, WA 98101
PHONE: 206.749.9000

VISIT OUR WEBSITE AT WWW.REALTIMEPERFORMANCE.COM

FIRST EBOOK EDITION: AUGUST 2009
FIRST PRINT EDITION: JANUARY 2010

ISBN: 978-0-615-31300-9

# Contents.

“Key leaders in business are in real need of a model – a roadmap – to guide effective employee development. The 5As Framework by Steve Gill and Sean Murray offers a simple, yet comprehensive description of the factors that lead to a learning culture. By not recognizing the impact of culture on learning, employee development will fail. Organizations and people applying this framework will take the needed steps to ensure that their training investments will produce desired business results.”

Winsor Jenkins, VP – Human Resources, Northwest Pipe Company and author, *The Collaborator: Discover Soccer as a Metaphor for Global Business Leadership*

The Opportunity.

# 1 Companies are not getting the desired performance improvement from their investment in learning interventions.

## The Opportunity

U.S. companies spend $134 billion annually on employee learning and development programs. If you were to interview, as we have, participants who have attended these programs, generally you would find they have a good time, enjoy meeting people from throughout the company, and appreciate a break from the normal routine. Many of these participants even pick up new skills and knowledge and, when pressed, will claim their experience was valuable and worthwhile. However, if you dig deeper, you will discover very few participants apply their learning to achieving important business goals.

In fact, research studies peg the average number of employees who apply what they learned to achieving business results at between 10% and 20% of participants in training programs. This means that 80% to 90% of participants are not applying the training in any significant way. If companies invested in training with the same rigor and analysis they apply to investing in equipment and software, there would be dozens of MBAs crawling through every training department in search of inefficiencies. Can you imagine, in this day and age, a manufacturing plant with a quality defect rate of 80%? But that is exactly the level of "quality" most organizations accept today in their training programs.

The average number of employees who apply what they learned to achieving business results is between 10% and 20% of participants in training programs.

## Missed Opportunity

If you talk with the 10% to 20% of managers who actually apply what they learned, you will find they often get tremendous results. One sales manager we interviewed who attended a relationship-selling workshop attributed newly-learned skills to closing a $15 million office systems deal with one of his customers. Consider, for a moment, that the relationship-selling course included nine other participants, each with territories and accounts similar in size to that of the successful sales rep. If everyone in the course was able to apply the new relationship selling skills to close a $15 million dollar deal, then at least theoretically, this company would generate an additional $135 million in revenue.

## One Learner Successfully Applied New Skills

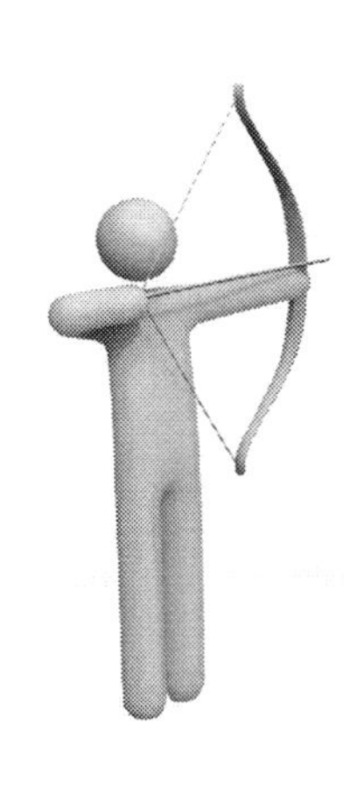

Result:

Closed an additional sale

Value to the organization:

# $15 million

## 9 Learners Were Unable to Successfully Apply New Skills

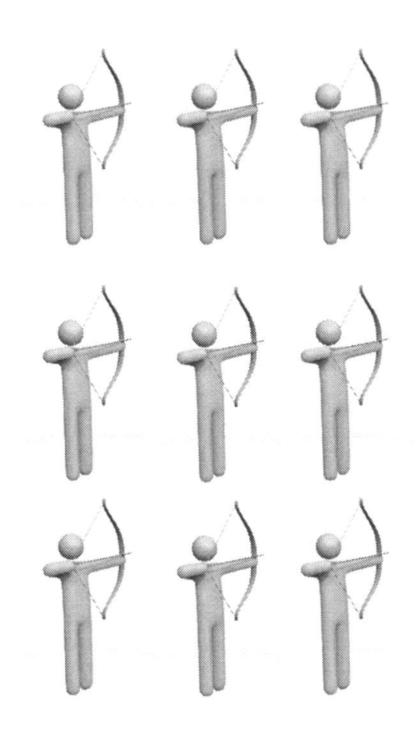

Result:

No measurable benefit to the organization

Value of missed opportunity:

# $135 million

If you are skeptical of this $135 million missed opportunity, assume for a moment that it is off by 10x. That is, the true missed opportunity here is closer to $13.5 million. Does that not still warrant further investigation and beg the questions: What about all of the other sales managers who could be getting that kind of result and are not? Were they not at the same training? Did they not experience the same quality learning event? What is preventing these learners from applying their new skills to achieve business results?

In most cases, organizational factors are the barriers to learning and change, not poor instructional design.

## Organizational Factors

When trying to determine why learners are not successfully applying what they learn, training departments often turn to the training event itself. We have all heard excuses about mediocre facilitators, poorly designed content and useless exercises. However, from our research, most participants find today's learning events highly engaging and educational. When we ask learners what is preventing them from being successful, most point to organizational factors that reside largely outside of the classroom.

In this book we explain why organizations are failing to get the most they can from training and what they can do to fix the problem. And, we tell you from research and our own experience how to optimize your investment in training programs.

Notes

Organizational
Factors.

# Organizational Factors

The following real-life case studies highlight the important role organizational factors play in helping or preventing an employee from applying new skills toward achieving business goals.

"I told my boss the program was about how to get teamwork between departments. He said that he's tried that and it doesn't work here."
—*Sam*

## Sam's Story

Sam is a Systems Engineering Manager for a technology services company. He has been with the company for seven years and has eight systems engineers reporting to him within the mid-range commercial business group. His boss nominated Sam to attend the company's New Leader Development Program. Sam's boss didn't say much about his reasons, other than that this was a course that Sam hadn't attended yet and it looked like an opportunity for Sam to "sharpen" his leadership skills. Sam showed up at the first day of a three-day off-site workshop without a clear understanding of the purpose of the program and what he was supposed to learn and do differently. However, the facilitator was especially engaging and Sam had a "terrific experience." He met many new people from other functions and business units, and felt that he "learned a lot." At the end of the third day, Sam gave the workshop the highest rating on the evaluation questionnaire.

"I liked the leadership program. It was great finally meeting people from other parts of the company. But I can't say anything has changed."

*-Sam*

Immediately upon returning to his office, Sam told his boss about how the workshop emphasized the value of cross-functional teamwork. Sam's boss responded by warning him that trying to collaborate with the Marketing and Sales groups would be a waste of time. Sam's boss pessimistically stated that those departments don't understand systems engineering—and furthermore, his previous attempts at collaboration with Sales and Marketing had failed. After that remark, Sam didn't try to apply any of the content from the New Leader Development Program.

When interviewed about the program six months later, Sam could not recall anything that he had done differently since participating in the Program that had contributed to enhanced business results for his business unit or for the company.

"I've been having some trouble with a couple people on my team. My boss said she hoped I would learn some ways to relate better to them and, possibly, not have to fire them. I agreed that this would be a good goal for me."

*-Carla*

## Carla's Story

Carla is the shift supervisor for a call center at a large hotel. She supervises three to four people each shift. In many cases, Carla and her employees are the first people to have contact with the property's guests. Carla was asked to attend the company's new three-day diversity workshop. Before going to the program, Carla met with her boss, who had already participated in the workshop, to discuss how the experience could benefit Carla, her team, and the hotel. Together, they identified some goals and outcomes that would contribute to their success.

The workshop was a powerful, life-changing experience for Carla. She discovered some blind-spots in her treatment of others. After the workshop, she met with her boss again and they

"I learned to listen before making a judgment, and a better way of giving feedback. After the workshop, I met with the problem employees and everything went much better."

*-Carla*

talked about applying what Carla had learned in the workshop to making her team more effective. These goals were made part of Carla's performance review. One example of learning was Carla's interaction with an employee who had a "smart mouth" and a "bad attitude" talking to guests on the phone. Before attending the diversity workshop, Carla was on the verge of firing this employee. After the workshop, Carla agreed with her boss to change her approach and give the employee another chance. She met with the employee, praised her first for the things she had done right, gave her feedback, and then asked her about what kind of help she needed. The employee confided in her saying, "I learn differently than other people." Carla discovered that all of the bravado and "over-talking" was the employee's way of compensating for her difficulties. Once this came out, Carla was able to figure out how to help this employee become successful. Now they work well together and the employee has become one of Carla's best operators. Carla successfully retained a valuable employee.

## Beyond Training

Conditions outside of the learning event determine the impact on business results.

Sam and Carla are examples of how organizational factors affect the impact of training. In terms of content and process, the New Leader Development Program attended by Sam and the Diversity Workshop attended by Carla were both exceptional programs. Each event met the highest standards for adult learning. The programs had clear, meaningful goals, interactive and engaging facilitation, opportunities for participants to share individual experiences, and small team interaction to build interest and commitment. These learning events received very high ratings from participants. Even so, our stories of Sam and Carla show how factors beyond the workshop made all the difference. Sam was unable to achieve any significant business results while Carla applied her new skills to retain a valuable employee.

When we ask managers why relatively few people are showing evidence of success from training, they mention conditions outside of the learning event, such as:

- Senior management does not understand the value of training.
- Our training department is not involved in strategic business planning.
- Our training budget has been cut severely.
- Employees are not learning what they need to learn to be successful.
- Training programs are isolated events with little follow-up.
- Employees are not given the opportunity to apply everything they learn in training.
- We don't have a way of measuring the extent to which training is having a positive impact on our organization.

# Before, During, and After Learning Interventions

We have evaluated the results of some of the best leadership development, business acumen, team building, and supervision skills programs in the field and it is always the same. Unless something is done before, during, and after the program to support learning and its application, there is very little impact on the bottom-line of a business. What we are suggesting here goes way beyond a little pre-training information packet and post-training reflection. Organizations must confront all of the factors that prevent learning from contributing to business success.

Adults do not learn in a vacuum. They need to believe that they can improve and they

Organizations must confront all of the factors that prevent learning from contributing to business success.

need to believe that what is being taught will be useful to them. They need to care about the knowledge and skills they are learning. They need to practice what they've learned soon after being exposed to the new material, and do this in an environment where they won't be criticized for being less than perfect. They need to apply the knowledge and skills to meaningful work. They need feedback. They need to feel recognized for what they have learned. And finally, they need to see meaningful results from their actions.

Imagine taking a golf lesson without being committed to improving your golf game. Or imagine not picking up a club again for months after the lesson, or, when you do play again, not keeping score and not having anyone observe your game and give you feedback. It's unlikely you would improve your game very much. You might remember a few things from the lesson that could help your game, but you would not be maximizing the value of the lesson. You would probably be better off skipping the lesson altogether and avoiding the frustration. Even if Tiger Woods was the instructor, you wouldn't learn very much.

However, this is what managers are often asked to do. They are asked to attend leadership training and development programs with little preparation, little support, minimal practice, no follow-up, and no feedback. And then the program is blamed for not bringing about the change that is needed.

Too often managers find themselves being parachuted into an instructional drop-zone. All of a sudden they are tapped to attend the latest and greatest training. Without preparation and without a plan for follow-up and follow-through, they are told to go to "Lean Manufacturing", "Seven Habits",

"Good to Great", "Customer Loyalty", "One Minute Manager", or some other "hot" program. Most "hot" programs offer useful content that would benefit anyone, but they are wasted efforts if the other key elements of learning are not in place.

That is why these programs go from "hot" to "cold" so quickly, which causes the program-of-the-month phenomenon in organizations. Employees attend and maybe they enjoy the experience (especially if held at an attractive location) and, in the short term, report that the program was beneficial and they liked talking with the other participants. Then, over time, their behavior and, more importantly, organizational performance do not improve. Still wanting change, executives and the HR Department begin to look for the "next big thing."

Companies today can no longer afford to rely on these isolated events to make a difference, whether a one-day skill-building workshop, or a year-long leadership development institute. Maybe there was a time when companies could offer these events to employees without concern for results. Today, resources are too precious. You must make sure that you are maximizing the impact from every performance intervention.

# Wanted: A Learning Culture

This means that rather than a culture of events, you need a culture of learning, one that supports ongoing learning throughout your organization.

In a learning culture, the normal behaviors, customs, expectations, and goals are all oriented towards learning and performance improvement. After conducting hundreds of studies of the impact of performance improvement programs, we have concluded that to create and maintain this culture, five factors must be present:

Alignment
Anticipation
Alliance
Application
Accountability

We call these factors the 5As and we explore them further in each of the next five chapters.

# The Five Key Organizational Factors that Lead to Business Success from Training

## 1 Alignment
Align learning with strategic goals.

## 2 Anticipation
Anticipate success.

## 3 Alliance
Create a learning alliance between learner and boss.

## 4 Application
Apply learning immediately.

## 5 Accountability
Hold learner and organization accountable for business results.

Notes

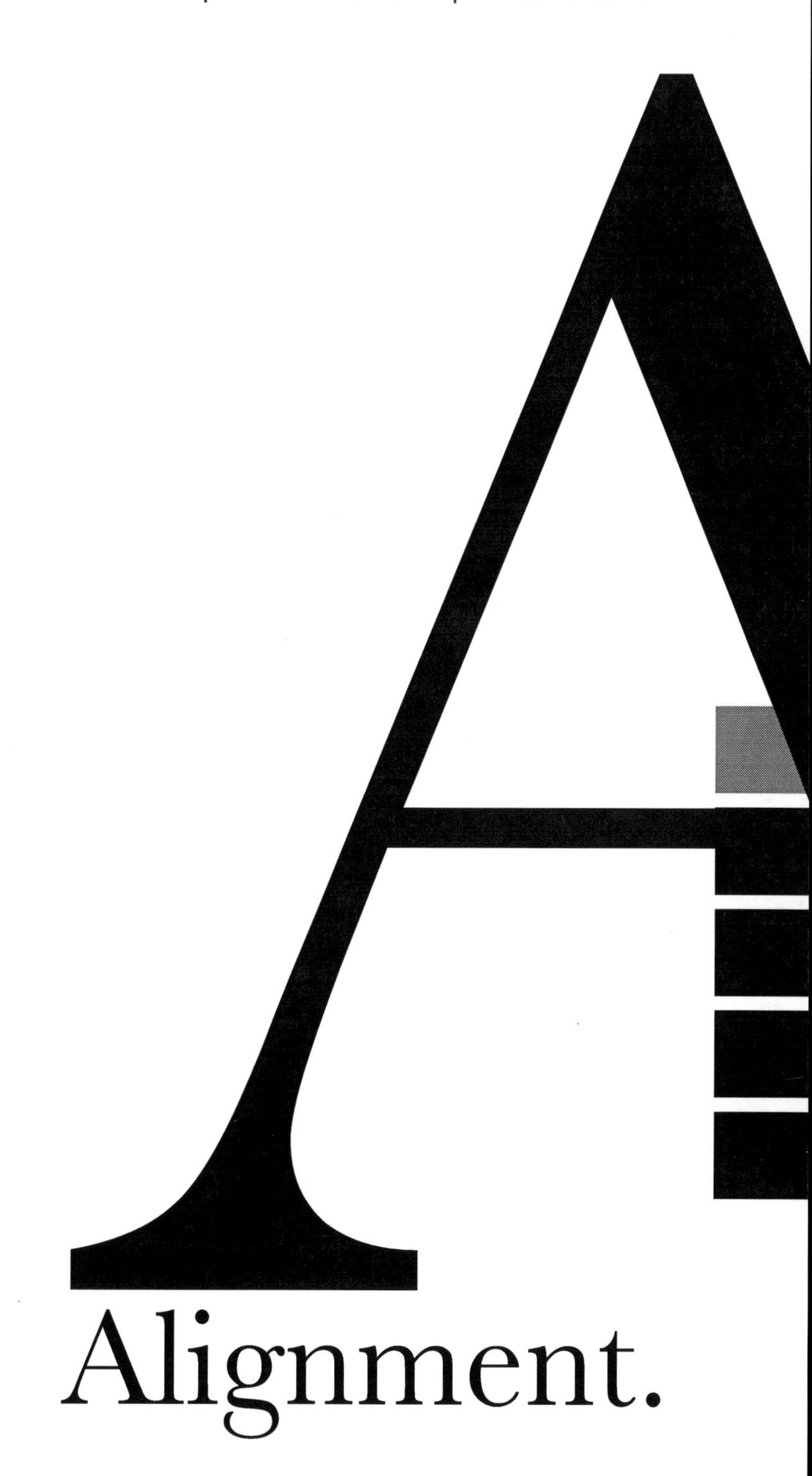

# Alignment.

# Alignment.

## Align learning with strategic goals.

# 3 Alignment is one of the five key factors that contribute to the success of any learning intervention.

## Alignment

Training has maximum impact when it is aligned with the business priorities of the organization. Like the archer who must have clear sight from bow to target, learners (and other learning stakeholders) must be clear about how the learning intervention will help them hit their business goals, such as increased revenue, decreased costs, greater market share, and compliance with regulations and standards.

Training and development activities must have an obvious link in the chain of value that results in significant, bottom-line performance outcomes.

Managers are more likely to learn and apply what they learn when they clearly understand how their participation in a learning intervention will help them be more effective leaders in their organizations. In other words, training and development activities must have an obvious link in the chain of value that results in significant, bottom-line performance outcomes. It might be nice to get together with other managers from time to time and participate in interesting experiences, but unless these events have an obvious relationship to business improvement, employees will not value learning from these experiences. It must be clear to learners that the knowledge, skills, attitudes, and beliefs they are being asked to internalize will contribute to their effectiveness in achieving outcomes for which they are held accountable.

## With alignment comes:

- a higher level of motivation
- greater commitment to results
- and a better understanding of what must be done to achieve success.

# Creating Alignment

Learners must be clear about how training will help them achieve their goals.

A bio-medical device company required all managers to attend a one-day workshop about the values and culture of the company. Many of the managers were less than enthusiastic and some considered it a waste of time. The HR department believed that this program was needed because of widespread confusion about the company's future direction. The organization had grown in size and complexity via mergers and

> acquisitions. As a result, each major division in the company had its own beliefs and practices. Management wanted to create a common set of values and a common culture among business units. The workshop was intended to contribute to these goals. It wasn't until the links between the workshop and culture change and between culture change and business results were made explicit that managers became motivated to participate.

Alignment is not static. The UK's Chartered Institute of Personnel and Development (CIPD) studies the mechanisms that affect training, learning, and development of people in organizations. They drew this conclusion about alignment:

> *The pursuit of alignment gives a clear direction to learning, training and development and ensures that a drift away from the strategic priorities of the organization does not occur...Alignment is both an outcome and a process. Alignment to a specific strategic or operational objective can be seen as an 'outcome' – something which is*

> *time-bound and measurable. On the other hand changes and developments in organizational priorities which occur in the fast-moving competitive environment in which many organizations operate means that alignment is also an ongoing process rather than a simple 'one-off' outcome.*

According to the CIPD, it's not enough to be able to describe the link between learning and results, one should also monitor and continuously improve this alignment over time and make adjustments as business priorities change.

Alignment is not about the training, per se. It's about what the organization as a whole needs to do to ensure that learners contribute to achieving strategic priorities. If I work for a hotel, how is what I'm learning today going to contribute to an increased occupancy rate? If I work for a bank, how is what I'm learning today going to contribute to an increase in deposits? If I work for a furniture manufacturer, how is what I'm learning today going to contribute to increased sales of office systems? When learning is aligned with strategic priorities, it's more likely that important business goals will be achieved, operational performance will improve, time and money for learning will be used efficiently, and talent will be developed over the long term.

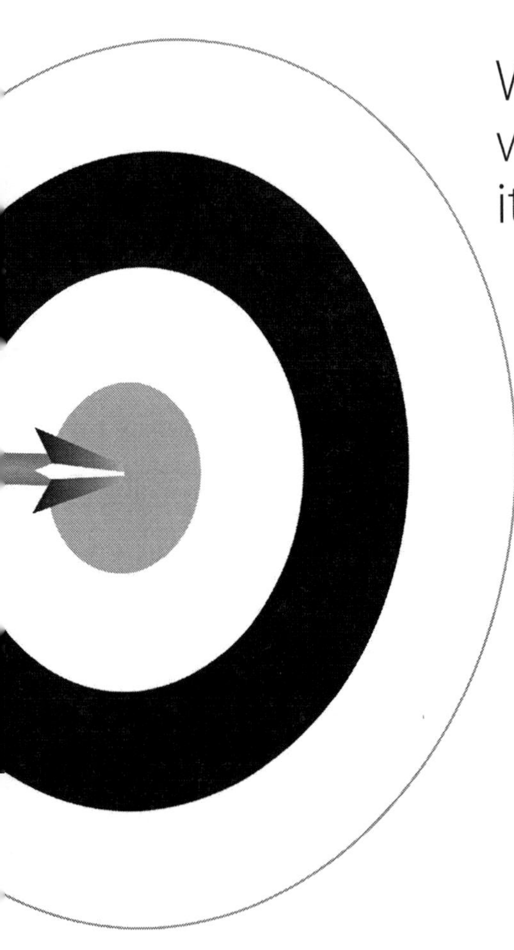

When learning is aligned with strategic priorities, it's more likely that

- Important business goals will be achieved .
- Operational performance will improve.
- Time and money for learning will be used efficiently.
- Talent will be developed over the long term.

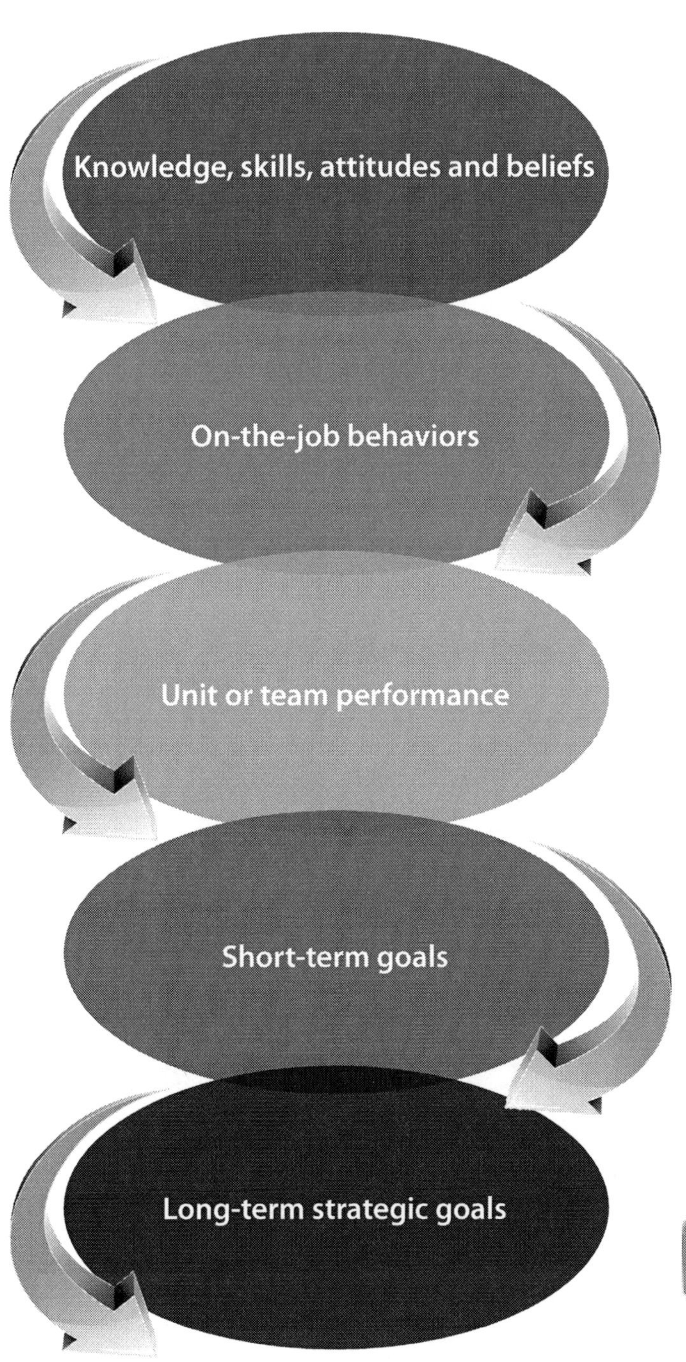


# Success Map

One way to achieve alignment is to create a map of the path from training to business success. We call this a "success map." Like a roadmap that visually shows you how to get from point A to point B with all of the landmarks along the way, a success map shows employees and the organizations how they will get from training to business success with indicators of progress.

Full-page template provided for print on page 117.

The Success Map provides the learner with a clear path connecting the learning event directly to the long-term strategic goals of the organization.

# Sales Training Success Map

You will probably be able to fill in much of this chart for your organization. That's the first step. To achieve alignment, however, all of the ovals in a Success Map must be interdependent. Taken together, they should describe the path from learning to business results and all of the key stops between. For example, a sales training program might look like this:

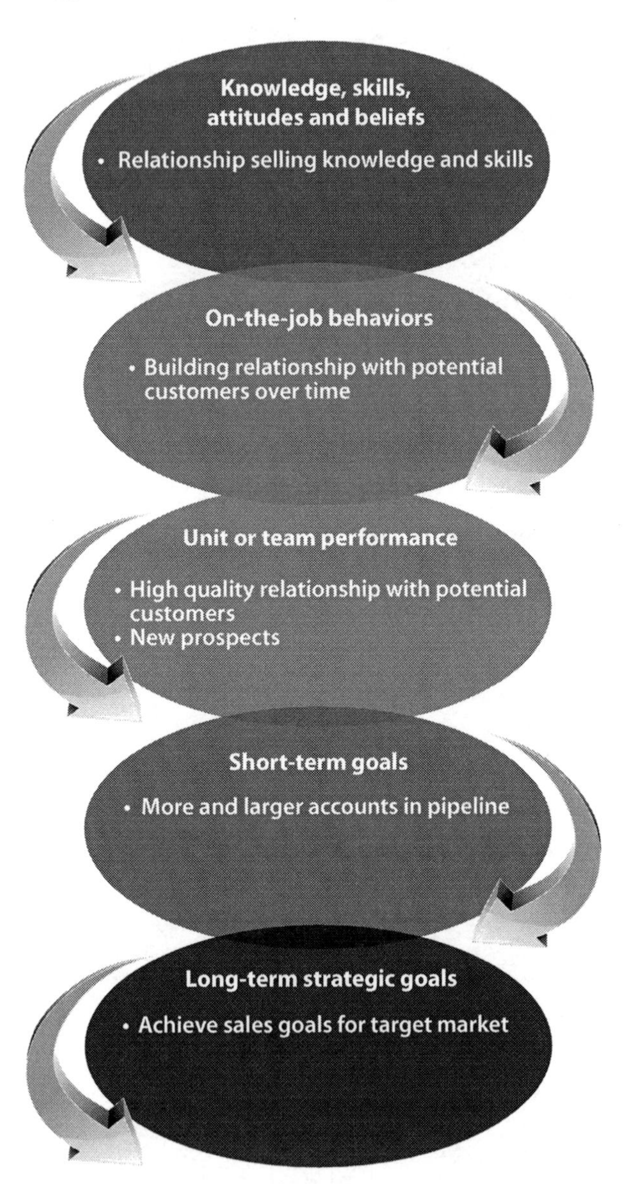


The Sales Training Success Map should describe the path from learning to business results and all of the key stops between.

Notes

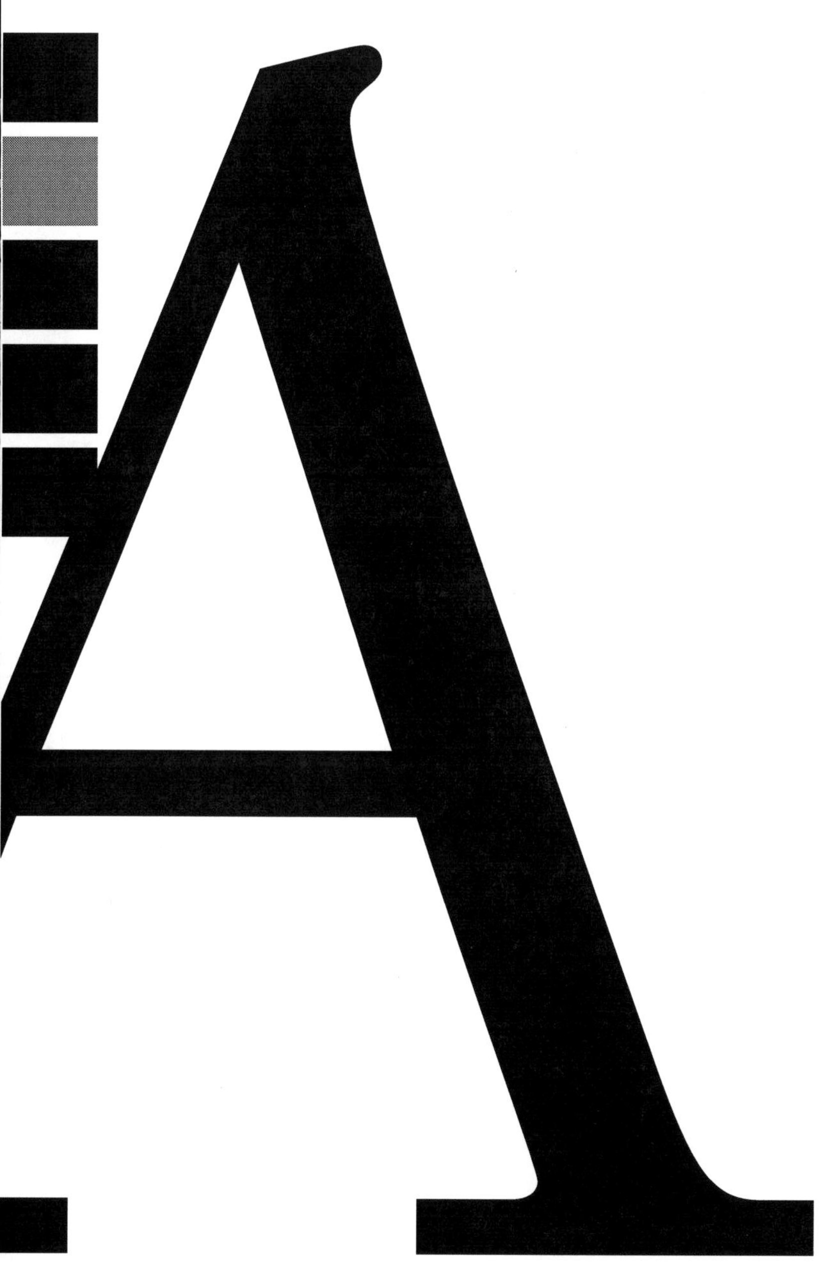

# Anticipation.

# Anticipation.

## Anticipate success.

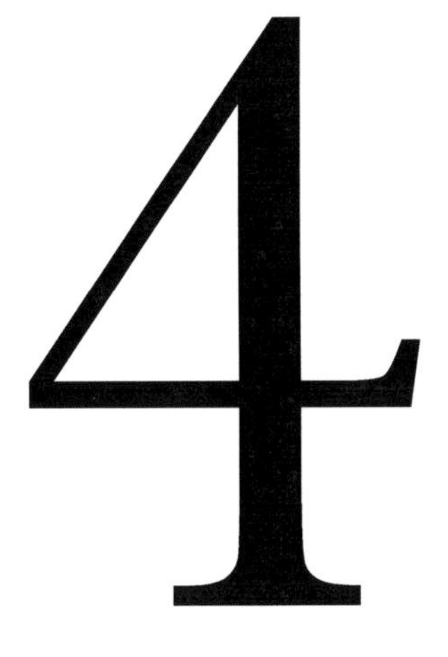

Even before the event, learners should be anticipating success.

# Anticipation

is another one of the five key organizational factors that affect the impact of training. Employees learn more when they anticipate success. They are more productive when they have high, but realistic, expectations for themselves. People who expect to increase their knowledge and skills learn more than people who do not have this expectation.

People who expect to increase their knowledge and skills learn more than people who do not have this expectation.

The research is very clear on this. What we expect of others and what others expect of themselves shapes their behavior, positively and negatively. Robert Rosenthal and Lenore Jacobson demonstrated this in their classic Pygmalion-effect study of teacher expectations of students' abilities. In their experiments, students whose teachers were told they were smart performed better than students whose teachers were told their students were not smart. Jane Elliott, in a classroom exercise, found that her students and then later, many adult workers, discriminated against each other simply because they were separated into either the brown-eyed, privileged group or the blue-eyed, disparaged group. This experiment showed that expectations shape discriminatory behavior. Rhona Weinstein, in her book, *Reaching Higher: The Power of Expectations in Schooling*, describes how expectations of teachers, as well as attitudes communicated by the school system, have a strong effect on student learning.

Employees who have a clear sense of the benefits and look forward to learning, are more likely to take full advantage of what the program offers from the outset.

Numerous studies that we have conducted on the impact of management development programs in companies have provided us with evidence that supports this notion of the power of expectations.

Employees who have a clear sense of the benefits and look forward to learning, are more likely to take full advantage of what the program offers from the outset. We have observed this in a wide variety of companies: high tech, manufacturing, shipping and trucking, cement and aggregates, and hospitality, among others.

## Maurice's Story

Maurice is the Quality Assurance manager for U.S. Aggregates, overseeing 22 QA technicians who are distributed among all of the different units in the company. The CEO of U.S. Aggregates sent a message to all managers that explained the purpose of a new management training program. He explained how the program would help everyone be more effective team leaders, improve safety in the plants, and produce higher quality product. Before attending the workshop, Maurice met with his boss to discuss the purpose of the course, prepare a Success Map together, and decide on Maurice's business goals for the program. They chose to focus on inventory reduction, which has a huge impact on available capital. Using the Success Map, they laid out how the training would result in Maurice enhancing his team leadership skills, which would result in better teamwork and more cross-functional sharing of information. This, in turn, would result in better planning of

"I've never expected much from management training programs in the past, but this time is different. I can see now how my training contributes to the success of our team."
*–Maurice*

> inventory and, finally, a significant reduction in inventory. The note from the CEO and the conversations with his boss shaped Maurice's expectations for the business goals he would achieve as a result of the training.

Even before employees participate in a learning event, they should be anticipating how they will benefit. They should think about what they will learn, why they will learn it, and what they will do with that learning after the event. For best results, employees should discuss and validate their expectations with their bosses. When learners and their bosses anticipate success, it is more likely that success will be the outcome.

Some companies have intentionally shaped expectations of their managers and bosses by including a pre-work phase in their management development programs. Prior to a multi-day, intensive, off-site workshop, these programs require participants to agree with their bosses on a business goal that they will achieve through the program. This process begins to shape expectations for what the participants will learn and be able to accomplish. We have found that learners who commit to ambitious but realistic business goals prior to workshops and courses tend to derive the most benefit from the experience.

## Options for Sending Senior Management Message:

- Email broadcast.
- Personal letter.
- Announcement at an all-employee meeting.
- Being present at the beginning of the training and kicking off the event.
- Video announcement on company intranet.

Employee expectations are shaped by the messages conveyed from senior management. Managers want to know that the training in which they will be participating is valued by the organization. Otherwise they will not be fully committed to the process and outcomes. "If the company doesn't care, why should I care?"

This message from senior management can be delivered in many different ways: an email broadcast; a personally addressed letter; announcement at an all employee meeting; senior manager being present at the beginning of the training; or a video announcement on the company intranet.

## Message from Senior Management

*"You have been selected to participate in Management Training II because you are one of the top performing managers in our company. We have high hopes for your future with us. I think MTII will help you become even more effective as a manager and a leader. I am confident that you will learn much from the program that you can apply immediately to your work. Please meet with your supervisor to discuss how your participation in the program will help your business unit and the company. If you have any questions about MTII, do not hesitate to contact your supervisor or HR."*

A sample message from Senior Management.

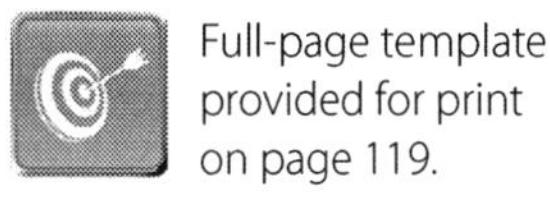
Full-page template provided for print on page 119.

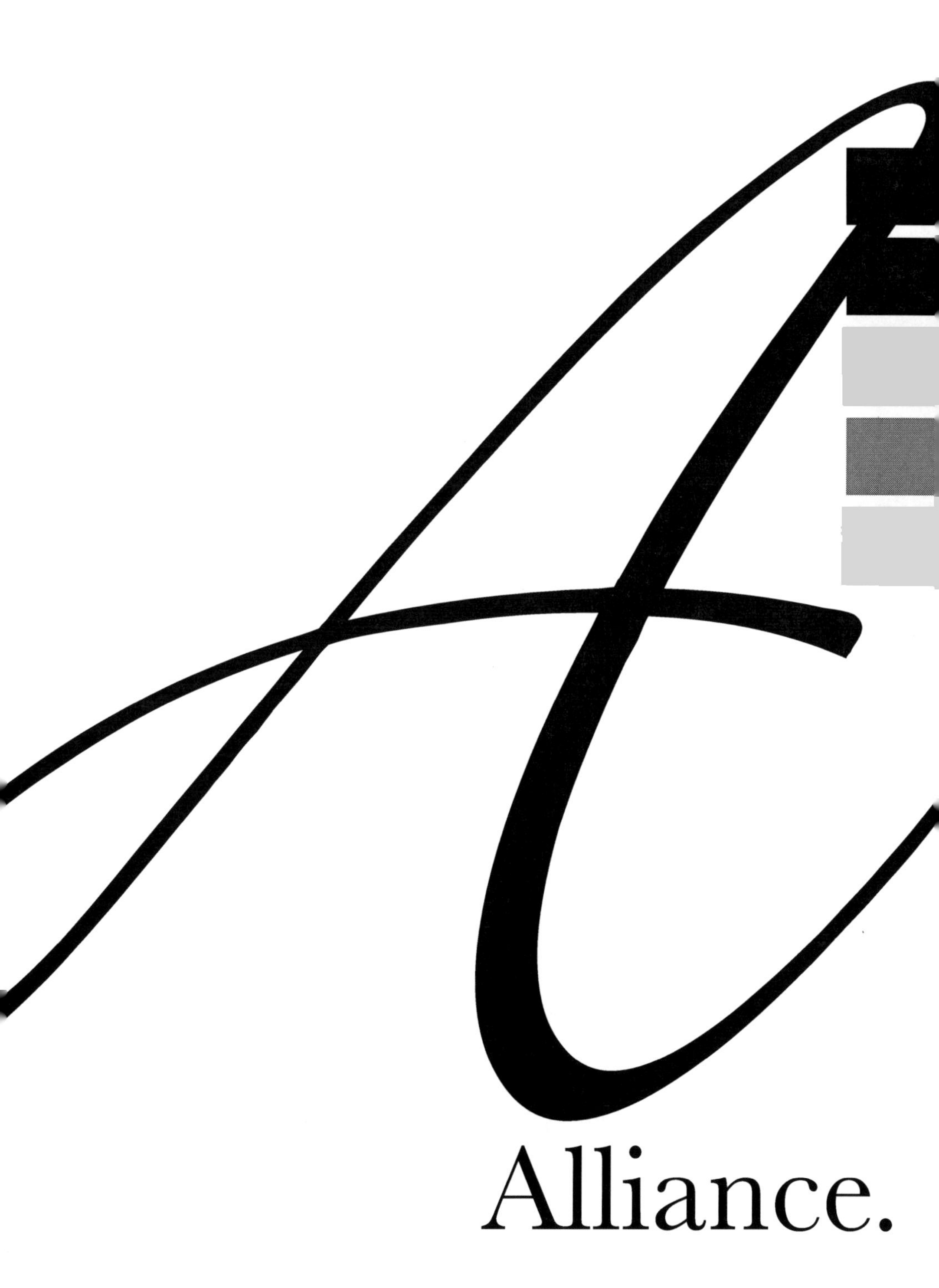

# Alliance.

# Alliance.

## Create learning alliance between learner and boss.

# 5 The establishment of a quality alliance between the learner and boss is essential.

## Alliance

An employee's supervisor and top level executives should be partners in the learning process. Supervisors play an essential role in working with learners to:

- Set goals (alignment).
- To clarify expectations (anticipation).
- To provide opportunities for utilization (application) of that learning on the job.
- And to determine impact (accountability).

And executives play an essential role in motivating employees to learn by communicating a message that the particular learning is valued by the organization. An example of this is the story of Chang:

# Chang's Story

Chang is a manager in the sales organization of a global high tech company. His boss asked him to attend the company's week-long leadership program for high potential managers. Initially, Chang was thrilled to be selected into the high potential program, but he was also anxious about spending a week away from his job, not making progress toward his annual goals. However, before the program began, Chang met with his boss to select a meaningful business objective to which he could apply training during and after the workshop. They chose the roll out of a new initiative to consolidate 34 distribution warehouses into one, regional warehouse. Chang and his boss discussed how the skills taught at the workshop could be applied specifically to the warehouse consolidation project. For one thing, Chang knew he needed to "get everyone onboard" because this was a major cultural change for the organization.

"It was nice to be selected for management training, but all I could think about were the projects on my plate."
*–Chang*

The discussions Chang had with his boss helped put the workshop in perspective. Chang no longer viewed the training as time away from his job, and instead saw it as an opportunity to help the company achieve success with a critical project. At the workshop, Chang was excited to discover that many of the new leadership skills he was learning could be applied to the warehouse project. The workshop prepared him by teaching him much about himself and how he could be a catalyst for large-scale change.

Chang no longer viewed the training as time away from his job, and instead saw it as an opportunity to help the company achieve success with a critical project.

Upon returning from the workshop, Chang met with his boss again to brief him on the new skills and knowledge he acquired and share an action plan for how he intended to apply these skills toward the warehouse consolidation project. As the project got started, he continued to revise the details of his business objective in discussions with his boss, and in return his boss provided valuable feedback. Even though Chang has had several different bosses while working on this project, he convinced each new boss of the importance of the project and gained that boss's support.

Chang opened the new distribution warehouse successfully and is looking to do a similar consolidation in other sales regions.

We have observed that the managers who learn the most from leadership development programs and do the most with what they have learned (i.e., produce business results) are the same managers who report that they met with their supervisors before and after the learning event to discuss goals and results. These are the managers who feel supported, who believe that their participation in the learning event is important to the organization, and believe that what they do afterwards to improve performance will be recognized and rewarded.

Learning in organizations should not be a solitary activity, at least not if you want employees to apply what they learned to their work and to achieving the strategic goals of the organization.

> Tim Mooney and Rob Brinkerhoff write in their book *Courageous Training*:
>
> *Training cannot succeed unless there is consistent commitment and action from several of the nontraining parts of the organization. Managers of trainees, for example, must provide the support, encouragement, and expectation for accountability so that employees try out training-acquired capabilities. Senior leaders must buy into and express a belief in the direction that training is steering toward. They must do this not only with words but also with actions. (p.28)*

Employees need a learning partner. This will usually be a boss or supervisor. Together, they should come to agreement about what is to be learned, why it is to be learned, and how the employee will apply the new knowledge or skills. The boss should serve in a coaching role, guiding the learner to maximize opportunity for success.

The learner and boss should work toward these goals together—in alliance. They should have regular conversations about what the learner should be getting out of the training and how it will be applied to achieve intended work outcomes and contribute to achieve business goals.

Evidence strongly suggests that this alliance between employee and supervisor has a positive effect on employee engagement. Tony Schwartz wrote this in ***Fast Company***:*

> *The single most important variable in employee productivity and loyalty turns out to be not pay or perks or benefits or workplace environment. Rather, according to the Gallup Organization, it's the quality of the relationship between employees and their direct supervisors. More*

* http://www.fastcompany.com/magazine/40/tschwartz.html

The learner and boss should work toward these goals together—in alliance. They should have consistent communication about:

- What the learner should be getting out of the training.
- How the training will be applied to achieve intended work outcomes.
- How the training will contribute to achieve business goals.

*specifically, what people want most from their supervisors is the same thing that kids want most from their parents: someone who sets clear and consistent expectations, cares for them, values their unique qualities, and encourages and supports their growth and development.*

This observation is supported by many studies that we have conducted on the impact of management and leadership training programs in companies. These studies consistently show that the relationship between learner and direct supervisor is critical to achieving important business goals.

A tool that can be used to guide this alliance is a list of seven steps that bosses can take to support learning. That list is shown on the next two pages.

# Steps Bosses Take to Support Learning

1

**STEP ONE:**
Discuss what the learner needs to learn in order to help your business unit achieve its objectives and the organization's strategic goals.

2

**STEP TWO:**
Agree on a set of learning objectives for the short-term and long-term.

3

**STEP THREE:**
Agree on the indicators that will be used to determine progress toward those objectives and achievement of goals.

4

**STEP FOUR:**
Describe how the learner can get the most out of the learning intervention.

5

## STEP FIVE:

Arrange for the learner to get whatever resources he or she needs to apply the learning to your business unit.

6

## STEP SIX:

Plan regular meetings (they may be brief) to discuss progress toward objectives and goals and any changes that would help the learner's progress.

7

## STEP SEVEN:

Make modifications in the learning intervention as needed.

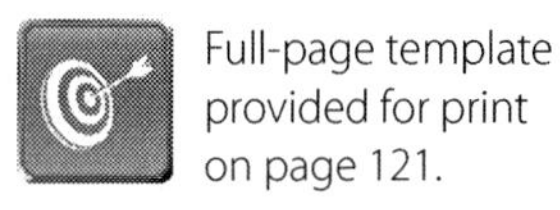
Full-page template provided for print on page 121.

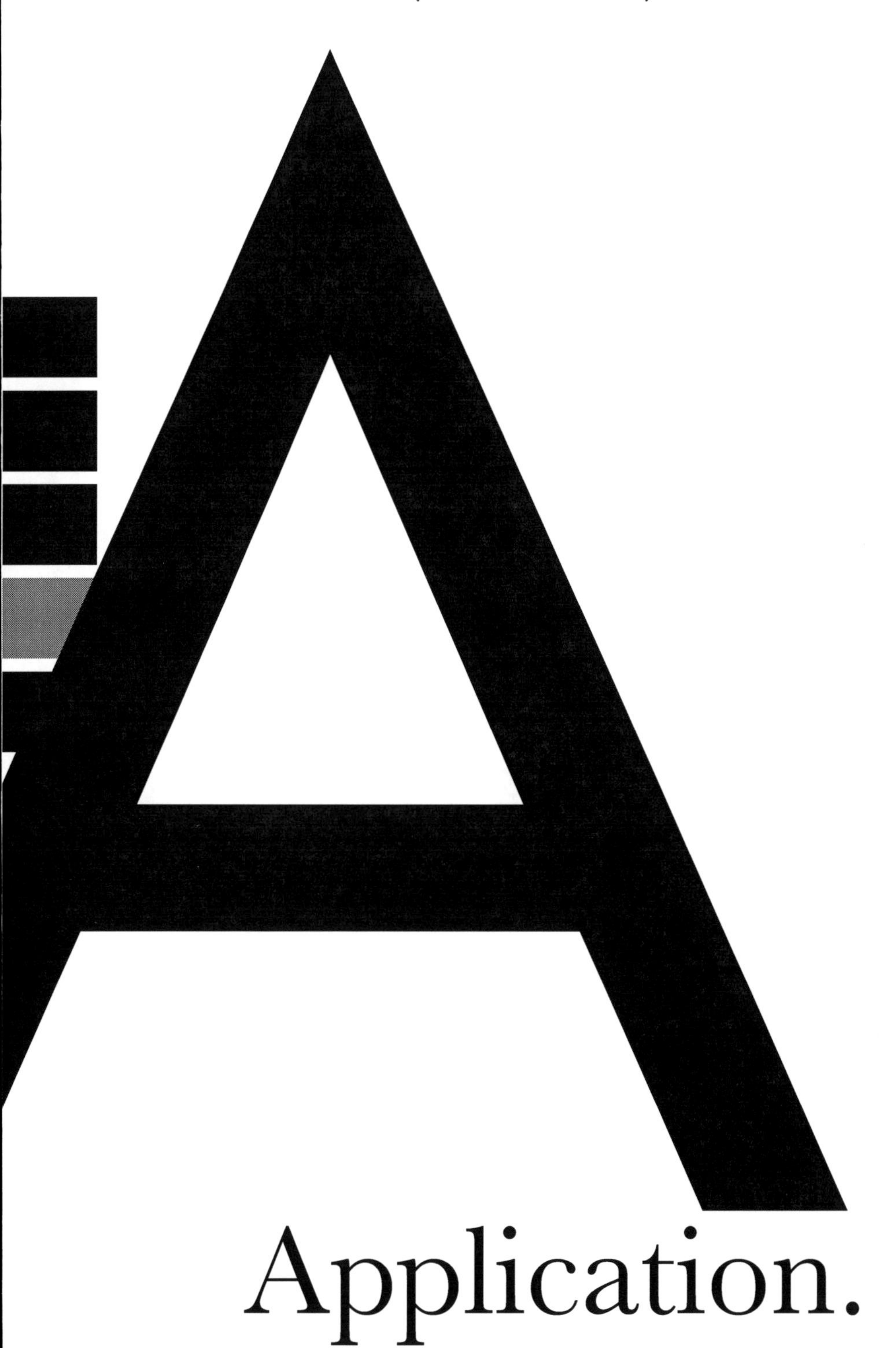

# Application.

# Application.

Apply learning immediately.

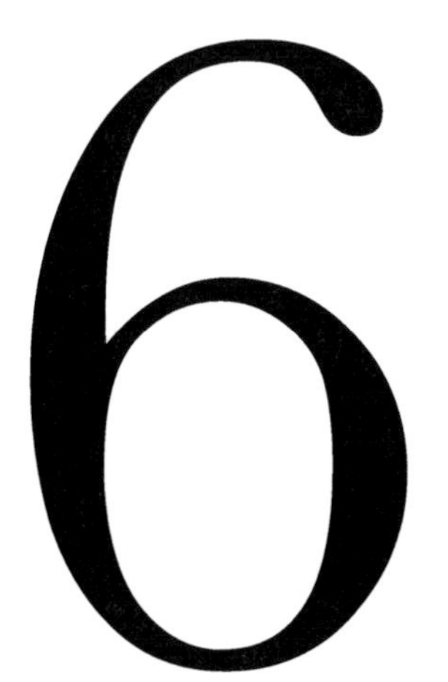

# Identify opportunities to apply learning shortly after the training event.

## Application

We know that for people to retain newly learned knowledge and skills they must apply that knowledge and those skills soon after learning. Whether building a team or solving a process problem, application of new knowledge and skills should occur within hours and days of the learning event, not within weeks and months, or never, as so often happens. This means that learners must have opportunities to apply what they have learned. Supervisors and bosses must encourage and support application of learning. And finally, learners and supervisors must plan ahead together to ensure that there will be opportunities for application. An example is Mark's story.

## Mark's Story

Mark is a senior sales manager for a hotel-casino in the U.S. He attended a three-day diversity workshop offered by his company. Since then, Mark has been applying the skills from the program as he says, "minute by minute." Because his business unit has to deal with people from all over the world, they have to be very careful, on a daily basis, to clarify mutual understanding. This is one of the skills Mark learned in the workshop. He had the opportunity to apply this newly learned skill almost immediately upon returning to his office. He arranges wholesale room contracts with sales people in India. He realized that sales managers in India interpret contracts differently than do sales managers in the U.S. If he gives someone in India 100 hotel rooms to sell, to Mark that means that contractually the person in India has to sell at least 80% of those rooms. However, in India, 80% is just a guideline. Sales people there assume that long term relationships are

Application of new knowledge and skills should occur within hours and days of the learning event, not within weeks and months, or never, as so often happens.

more important than any short-term goal. Mark realized from the diversity workshop that he has to let his customers (sales people in India) know how he views the contract and do this in a way that is not insulting. He immediately changed the way he relates to his customer in India. Now, when Mark talks to a customer in India about contracts, he will say something like, "This is how I see it. You seem to see it differently. We need to solve this problem together." This approach saved at least one contract worth more than $25,000 to Mark's business unit and, more importantly, it saved a long term business relationship with a valued customer.

The opportunity to use newly acquired skills cannot be left to chance.

Part of the reason Mark was effective in this situation was that the opportunity to apply his new learning occurred shortly after he participated in the diversity workshop. Fortunately for Mark, these opportunities occur for him on a daily basis. He was able to apply his new knowledge and skills before losing this ability to time. But the opportunity to use newly acquired skills cannot be left to chance. Trainees and managers need to search out and identify important situations where the employee can use these new skills.

Trainees and managers need to search out and identify important situations where the employee can use these new skills.

A tool that can help learning partners in this process is an Individualized Learning Plan. This is a document that says:

- What will be learned and how this learning will be applied to achieve results.
- What resources will be needed to be successful.
- Who should be involved in helping the learner.
- Target dates for reaching goals.
- How performance will be measured.

The ILP should be developed over the course of a series of conversations between learning partners. See an example of an Individualized Learning Plan Checklist on the next pages.

# Individualized Learning Plan Checklist

## Before the learning event, the learner:

- [ ] Understands how his or her performance must change to help the organization achieve its goals.

- [ ] Understands the goals and objectives of the learning intervention.

- [ ] Has reasonable expectations for his or her own performance during and after the learning intervention.

- [ ] Arranges an opportunity to apply the new knowledge, skills, beliefs, and attitudes immediately after the intervention.

- [ ] Is aware of organizational support and encouragement for learning and performance improvement.

## During the learning event, the learner:

- ☐ Understands what he or she will have to do to apply the new knowledge, skills, beliefs, and attitudes to the workplace.
- ☐ Explains what he or she is learning to others.
- ☐ Practices the skills being taught during the event.
- ☐ Receives feedback on knowledge and skills.
- ☐ Is prepared for any obstacles in the workplace that might interfere with performance of the new skills.
- ☐ Feels support and encouragement for learning and performance improvement.

## After the learning event, the learner:

- [ ] Applies the new knowledge, skills, beliefs, and attitudes to work.
- [ ] Receives rewards for learning and application to work.
- [ ] Removes any obstacles to applying the learning.
- [ ] Receives feedback on how well he or she is performing.
- [ ] Understands additional learning needs and how to meet these needs.
- [ ] Understands how continuous learning will help the organization achieve its goals.
- [ ] Feels support and encouragement for continuous learning and performance improvement.

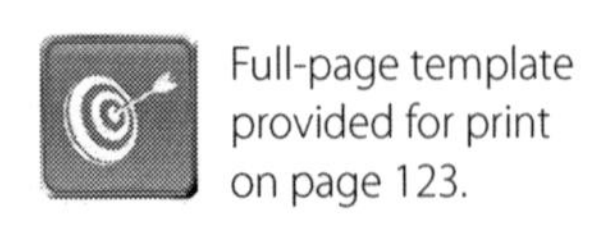
Full-page template provided for print on page 123.

Notes

# Accountability.

# Accountability.

## Hold learner and organization accountable for business results.

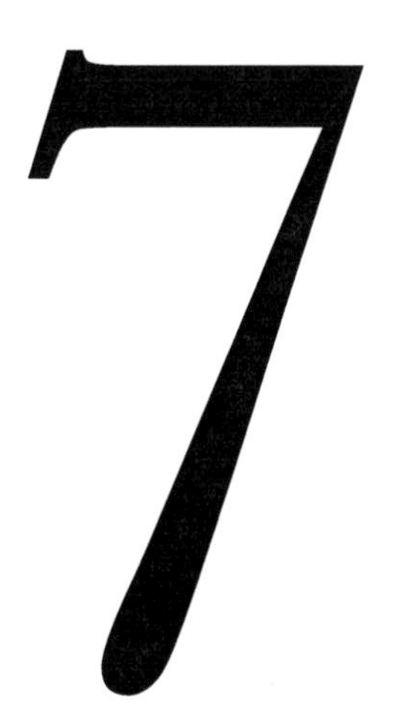

# 7 Learners must be held accountable for achieving results.

# Accountability

What happened as a result of the learning process? Did the learning contribute to important business results? Was it worth the time, effort, and cost? Would the business goals have been achieved

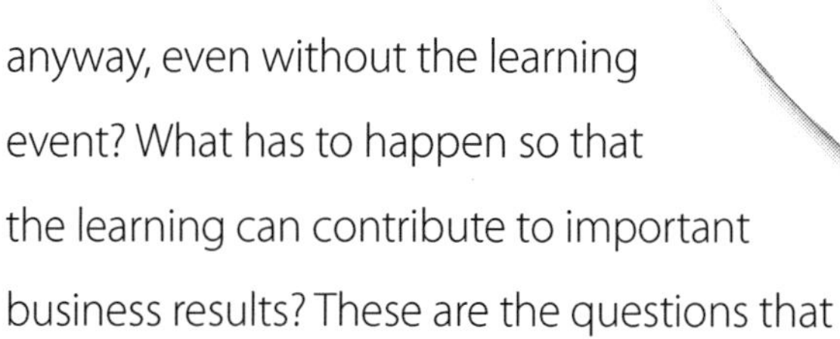

anyway, even without the learning event? What has to happen so that the learning can contribute to important business results? These are the questions that cause supervisors and learners to reflect on the learning process.

Answers to these questions tell learners where they are and what they still need to do to improve performance.

Without accountability, it's like playing golf in the dark. Players don't know if they hit the ball towards the pin and they don't know if they got the ball in the hole, and, after awhile, nobody cares. An example of accountability is the story of a shipping company:

We have found that asking managers about the impact of a leadership development program they attended is like a jump start for action.

A shipping company asked its executives to attend a workshop that had as its focus a business simulation. The purpose of the simulation was to help these executives develop their business acumen, network with other executives across the company, and examine their teamwork skills. At the conclusion of the simulation, participants were asked to develop a personal action plan that incorporated their learning from the program. These action plans contained commitments to operational improvements that drive profitability and could be implemented upon returning to the workplace. Each executive was reminded every three months to report progress on their action plans.

In this case, participants in the workshop were being held accountable for what they learned. This had the effect of keeping participants focused on results from the company's investment in their learning.

The process of being accountable can add tremendously to learning. Simply by asking people questions about what they learned and how they are applying what they learned, learners think and reflect about their experience. This can renew individual commitment to improve performance that might have been made at the time of the learning event but waned in the face of work responsibilities and pressures. We have found that asking managers about the impact of a leadership development program they attended is like a jump start for action. They frequently remember the changes they had intended to make after the program and then they re-commit to making those changes.

Learning, to be sustained, needs positive reinforcement. By bringing attention to the business results, rewarding successful performance, and showing your appreciation for what has been accomplished, you are reinforcing learning.

Accountability is also about recognizing, rewarding, and showing appreciation for achieving important business results.

Learning, to be sustained, needs positive reinforcement. By bringing attention to the business results, rewarding successful performance, and showing your appreciation for what has been accomplished, you are reinforcing learning.

Accountability can be achieved in many different ways. We have found that one of the most effective ways is to tell learners' success stories. We recommend first identifying employees who have achieved success after participating in the learning intervention and then interviewing those successful learners. Using the Success Map as a guide, ask them questions that will surface stories that start with their learning expectations, continue with their learning alliances, and end with business results. Quantify the impact, if possible, but it's the stories that will help you explain the business results from training and what can be done to achieve even greater success in the future. See Interview Guide on the next page.

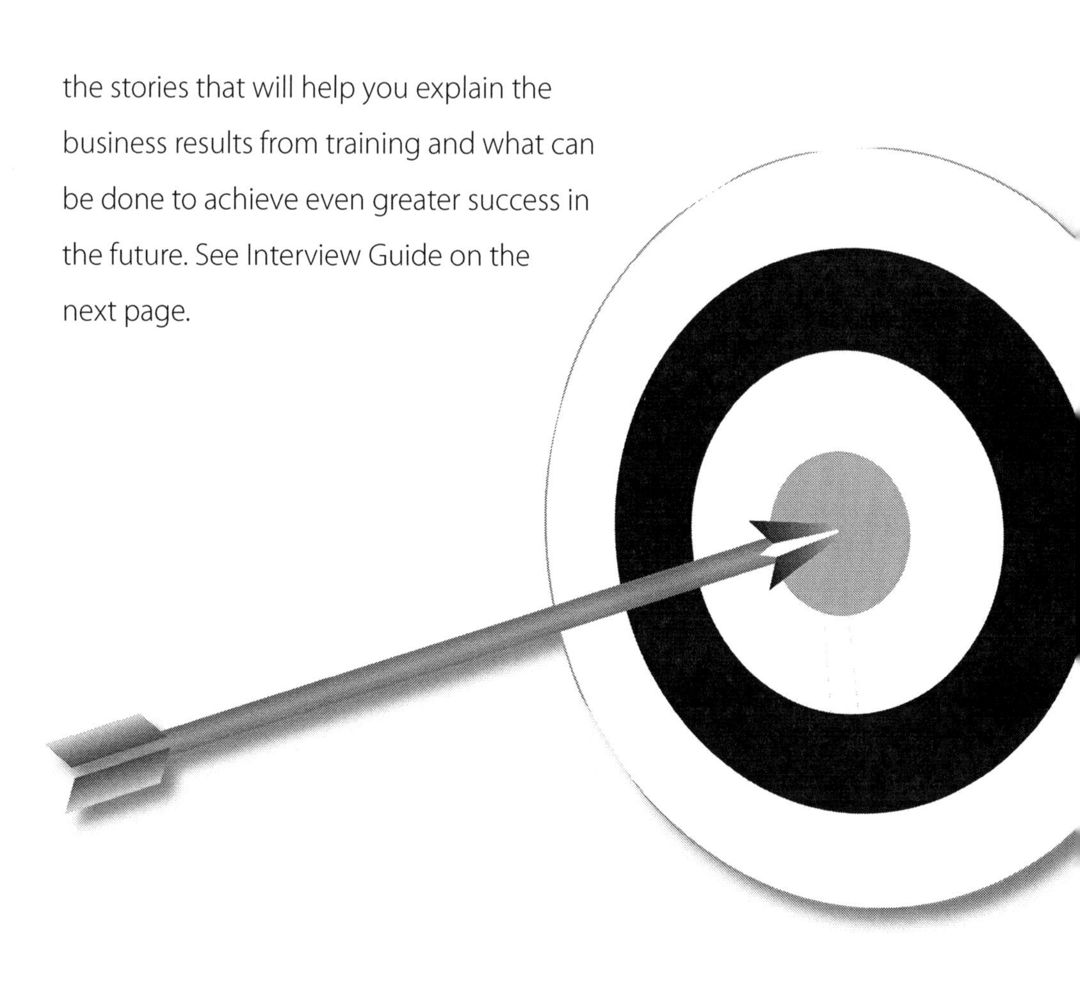

## Using the Success Map as a guide, ask questions that will surface stories that:

- Start with their learning expectations.
- Continue with their learning alliances.
- End with business results.

# Interview Guide

1. Ask learners about how they became involved in the program in the first place. Did they have a purpose for attending or was it simply a request by their bosses to attend? If there was a clear purpose, was it related to the organization's strategic goals? Knowing this will help to assess **Alignment**.

2. Ask learners about their expectations. What did they hope to learn from the program and how did they think that would help them in their work? Knowing this will help to assess **Anticipation**.

3. Ask learners about involvement of their bosses or supervisors. Did they discuss the program, what they would learn, and how that learning could be applied on the job? Knowing this will help to assess **Alliance**.

4 Ask learners about how they have used what they learned. What parts of the program helped them improve what they were doing in the workplace? What did they actually do that is different from what they were doing before? What obstacles did they face in trying to apply what they learned? Knowing this will help to assess **Application**.

5 Ask learners about impact. Did the program contribute to achieving important business results? What else could have been done to achieve even more impact from the program? Knowing this will help to assess **Accountability**.

Full-page template provided for print on page 125.

Business Results.

# Business Results

I'm sure you wish you could just send someone away to a workshop or class and then after a few days the

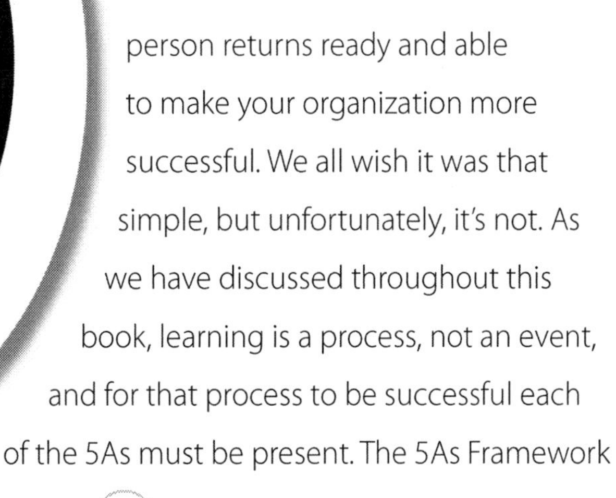

person returns ready and able to make your organization more successful. We all wish it was that simple, but unfortunately, it's not. As we have discussed throughout this book, learning is a process, not an event, and for that process to be successful each of the 5As must be present. The 5As Framework is a simple yet powerful model that applies systems thinking to the learning process. Although many of the examples in this book talk about applying the 5As Framework to an existing learning event, it can also be applied to the learning design process. The table below lists each of the 5As and a description of how they can be incorporated into the design of a new learning event.

## The 5As Framework Applied to Learning Design

| | |
|---|---|
| Alignment | Learning events are designed to transmit the knowledge, skills, attitudes, and beliefs that will logically result in the intended business impact. |
| Anticipation | Learners have realistic expectations for what they will learn and be able to do as a result of the program. |
| Alliance | Learners and their direct supervisors work together to maximize the impact of learning. |
| Application | Learners apply new knowledge, skills, attitudes, and beliefs to achieving business goals for themselves, their teams, and the organization. |
| Accountability | Learner performance is measured and learners are recognized,rewarded, and shown appreciation for applying new learning to achieving business goals. |

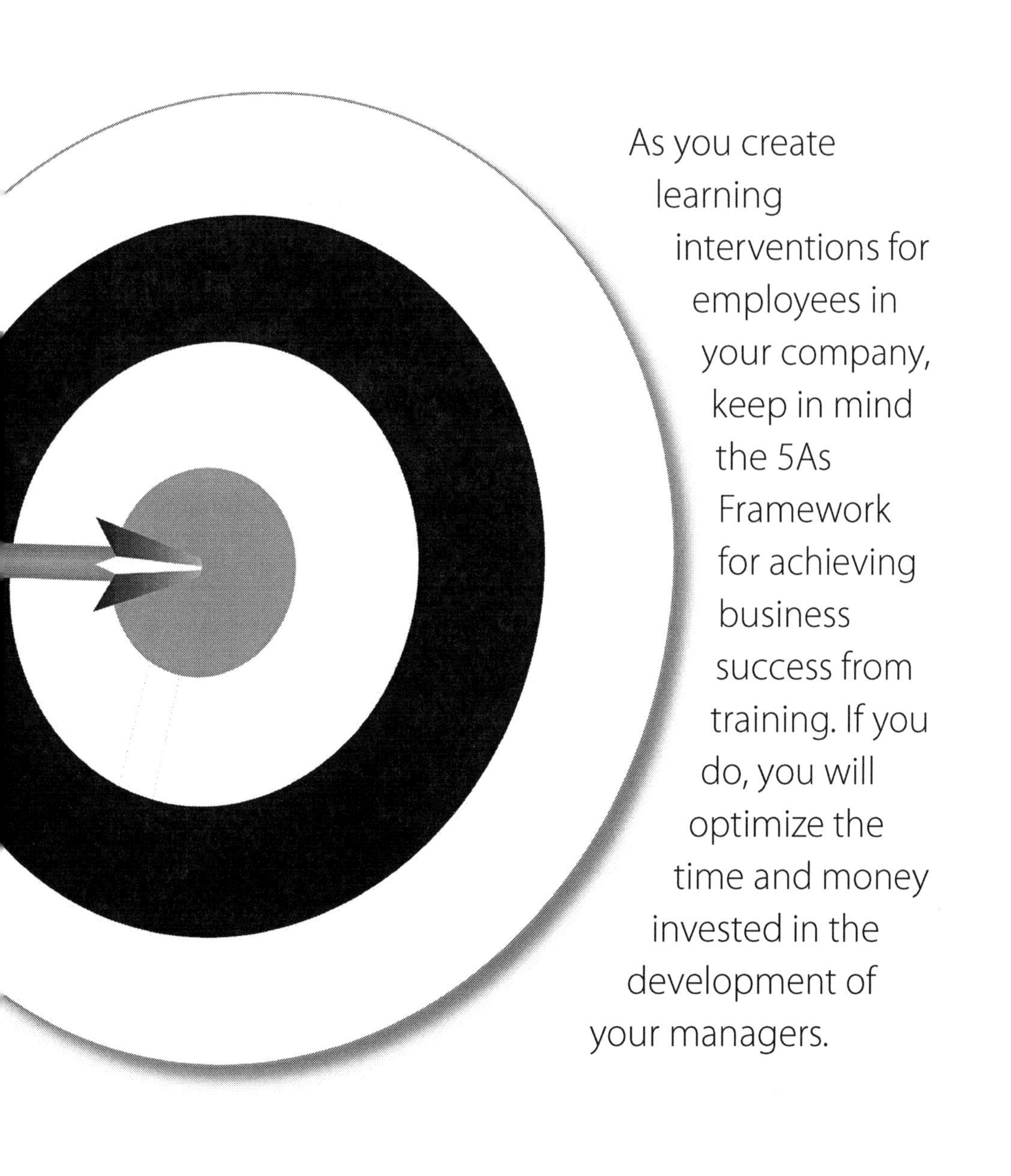

As you create learning interventions for employees in your company, keep in mind the 5As Framework for achieving business success from training. If you do, you will optimize the time and money invested in the development of your managers.

When implementing any learning intervention, whether that is an instructor-led course, elearning, coaching, video or audio materials, simulation, internship, or a program at a local college, use the 5As framework to ensure that learning is applied to achieving business results for your organization.

If you are a learner, ask your boss what you will do together for each of the 5As. If you are the boss of a learner, check with that person to ensure that each of the 5As is addressed. By doing this you increase the impact and optimize the value of your investment in training.

# 5As Framework Audit

One way to get started with implementing the 5As Framework at your organization is to perform a 5As Framework Audit. The purpose of this audit is to help organizations assess to what extent the 5As currently guide their learning interventions. It is always good to know where things stand today with respect to the 5As. Not only will this provide a baseline from which you can measure future progress, it will also help you prioritize where to invest your precious time and energy to get the best return.

- Is it clear to everyone how training contributes to achieving business goals (alignment)?
- Do learners and their managers have high expectations for what they will learn and apply (anticipation)?
- Is the involvement of managers with learners continuous throughout the learning process (alliance)?
- Do employees apply what they learned in training to achieving business goals (application)?
- Is there evidence of how training makes a difference in the organization (accountability)?

The 5As Framework Audit is provided on the following pages. You can fill this out on your own, or send it to others throughout your organization to get multiple perspectives.

# 5As Framework Audit

| FACTORS | QUESTIONS | RESPONSE |
|---|---|---|
| Alignment | 1. Learners know the strategic business goals of the organization. | YES/NO/Don't Know |
| | 2. It is likely that the learning intervention will result in performance improvement that will contribute to achieving these goals. | YES/NO/Don't Know |
| | 3. I can measure the strength of the relationship between the learning intervention and achieving business goals. | YES/NO/Don't Know |
| Anticipation | 4. Learners know what they will learn from the intervention. | YES/NO/Don't Know |
| | 5. Learners know what will change as a result of their learning. | YES/NO/Don't Know |
| | 6. Learners are enthusiastic about the opportunity to learn and perform differently in their jobs. | YES/NO/Don't Know |
| Alliance | 7. Supervisors/bosses of learners know what learners will learn and how that learning will be applied on-the-job. | YES/NO/Don't Know |
| | 8. Supervisors/bosses of learners meet with their direct reports to set performance goals for the learning intervention. | YES/NO/Don't Know |
| | 9. Supervisors/bosses of learners encourage and support learners as they participate in the learning intervention and attempt to apply new knowledge, skills, attitudes, and beliefs on-the-job. | YES/NO/Don't Know |

| FACTORS | QUESTIONS | RESPONSE |
| --- | --- | --- |
| Application | 10. Learners have the opportunity within 48 hours to apply new knowledge, skills, attitudes, and beliefs to achieving business goals for themselves, their teams, and the organization. | YES/NO/Don't Know |
| | 11. Learners have the resources they need to apply their learning. | YES/NO/Don't Know |
| | 12. Application of newly developed competencies is valued by the organization. | YES/NO/Don't Know |
| Accountability | 13. Impact of learning on achieving business goals is measured. | YES/NO/Don't Know |
| | 14. Learners are recognized and rewarded for applying new learning to achieve business goals. | YES/NO/Don't Know |
| | 15. Performance data is used to improve learning interventions and enhance impact. | YES/NO/Don't Know |

Review your answers.
What are the implications of your answers for learning in your organization? Which of the 5As is strong in your organization and which are weak? What would you like to change? How are you going to do that?

Full-page template provided for print on page 127.

# Tools.

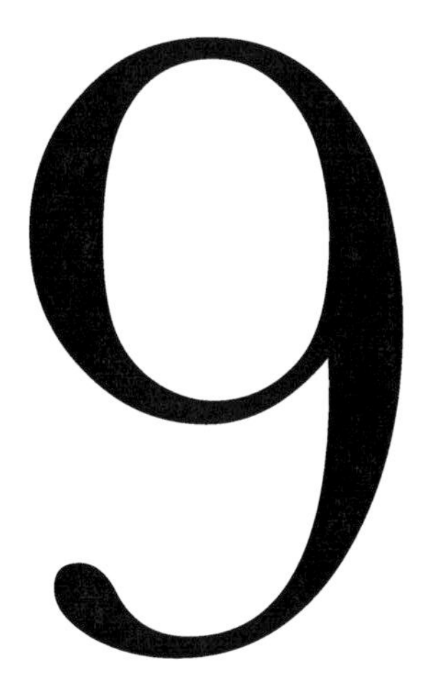

In this chapter we provide you with a tool for each of the 5As.

Use the

- Success Map Template to achieve Alignment.
- The Executive Message to shape Anticipation.
- Steps Bosses Take to Support Learning Alliance.
- The Individualized Learning Plan Checklist to ensure Application.
- The Interview Guide to maintain Accountability.
- The 5As Framework Audit to assess your organization on each of the five factors.

# Success Map Template

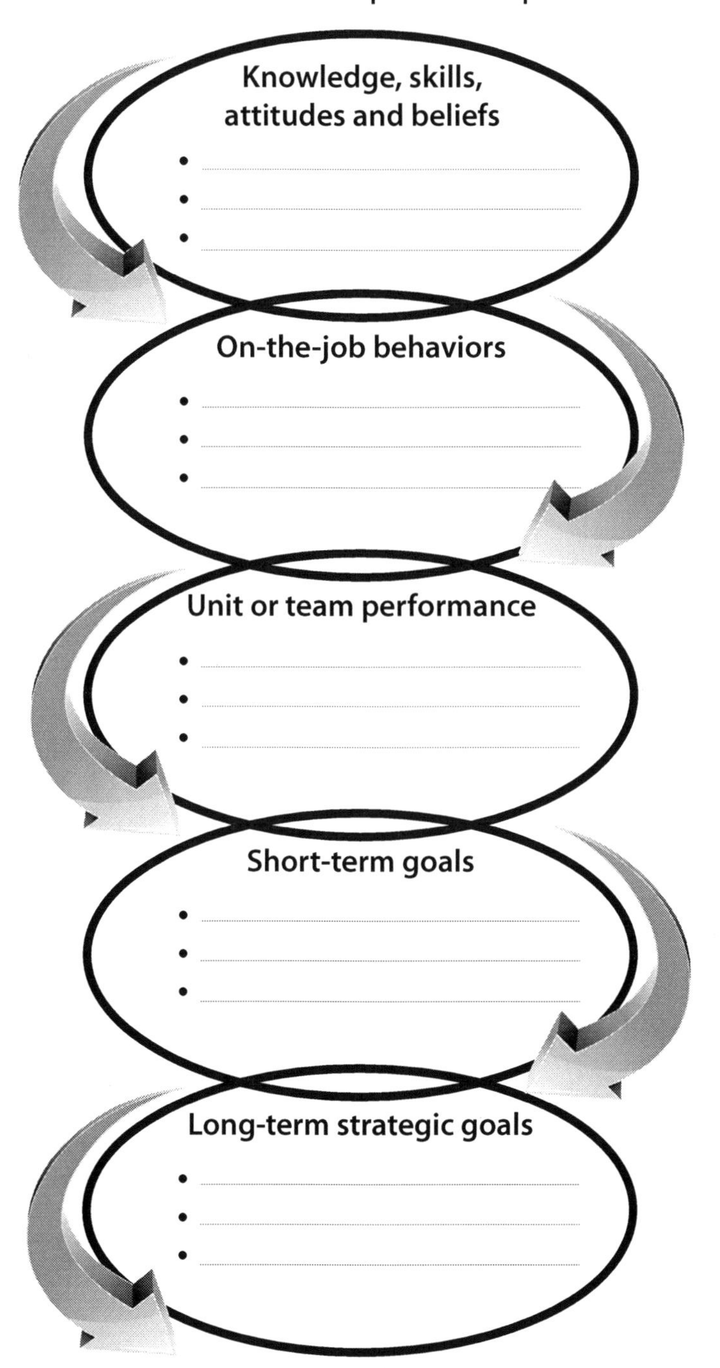

## Message from Senior Management

*"You have been selected to participate in Management Training II because you are one of the top performing managers in our company. We have high hopes for your future with us. I think MTII will help you become even more effective as a manager and a leader. I am confident that you will learn much from the program that you can apply immediately to your work. Please meet with your supervisor to discuss how your participation in the program will help your business unit and the company. If you have any questions about MTII, do not hesitate to contact your supervisor or HR."*

# Steps Bosses Take to Support Learning

1

**STEP ONE:**
Discuss what the learner needs to learn in order to help your business unit achieve its objectives and the organization's strategic goals.

2

**STEP TWO:**
Agree on a set of learning objectives for the short-term and long-term.

3

**STEP THREE:**
Agree on the indicators that will be used to determine progress toward those objectives and achievement of goals.

4

**STEP FOUR:**
Describe how the learner can get the most out of the learning intervention.

5

**STEP FIVE:**
Arrange for the learner to get whatever resources he or she needs to apply the learning to your business unit.

6

**STEP SIX:**
Plan regular meetings (they may be brief) to discuss progress toward objectives and goals and any changes that would help the learner's progress.

7

**STEP SEVEN:**
Make modifications in the learning intervention as needed.

# Individualized Learning Plan Checklist

## Before learning event, the learner:

- [ ] Understands how his or her performance must change to help the organization achieve its goals.
- [ ] Understands the goals and objectives of the learning intervention.
- [ ] Has reasonable expectations for his or her own performance during and after the learning intervention.
- [ ] Arranges an opportunity to apply the new knowledge, skills, beliefs, and attitudes immediately after the intervention.
- [ ] Is aware of organizational support and encouragement for learning and performance improvement.

## During the learning event, the learner:

- [ ] Understands what he or she will have to do to apply the new knowledge, skills, beliefs, and attitudes to the workplace.
- [ ] Explains what he or she is learning to others.
- [ ] Practices the skills being taught during the event.
- [ ] Receives feedback on knowledge and skills.
- [ ] Is prepared for any obstacles in the workplace that might interfere with performance of the new skills.
- [ ] Feels support and encouragement for learning and performance improvement.

## After the learning event, the learner:

- [ ] Applies the new knowledge, skills, beliefs, and attitudes to work.
- [ ] Receives rewards for learning and application to work.
- [ ] Removes any obstacles to applying the learning.
- [ ] Receives feedback on how well he or she is performing.
- [ ] Understands additional learning needs and how to meet these needs.
- [ ] Understands how continuous learning will help the organization achieve its goals.
- [ ] Feels support and encouragement for continuous learning and performance improvement.

# Interview Guide

1. Ask learners about how they became involved in the program in the first place. Did they have a purpose for attending or was it simply a request by their bosses to attend? If there was a clear purpose, was it related to the organization's strategic goals? Knowing this will help to assess **Alignment**.

2. Ask learners about their expectations. What did they hope to learn from the program and how did they think that would help them in their work? Knowing this will help to assess **Anticipation**.

3. Ask learners about involvement of their bosses or supervisors. Did they discuss the program, what they would learn, and how that learning could be applied on the job? Knowing this will help to assess **Alliance**.

4. Ask learners about how they have used what they learned. What parts of the program helped them improve what they were doing in the workplace? What did they actually do that is different from what they were doing before? What obstacles did they face in trying to apply what they learned? Knowing this will help to assess **Application**.

5. Ask learners about impact. Did the program contribute to achieving important business results? What else could have been done to achieve even more impact from the program? Knowing this will help to assess **Accountability**.

# 5As Framework Audit

| FACTORS | QUESTIONS | RESPONSE |
|---|---|---|
| Alignment | 1. Learners know the strategic business goals of the organization. | YES/NO/Don't Know |
| | 2. It is likely that the learning intervention will result in performance improvement that will contribute to achieving these goals. | YES/NO/Don't Know |
| | 3. I can measure the strength of the relationship between the learning intervention and achieving business goals. | YES/NO/Don't Know |
| Anticipation | 4. Learners know what they will learn from the intervention. | YES/NO/Don't Know |
| | 5. Learners know what will change as a result of their learning. | YES/NO/Don't Know |
| | 6. Learners are enthusiastic about the opportunity to learn and perform differently in their jobs. | YES/NO/Don't Know |
| Alliance | 7. Supervisors/bosses of learners know what learners will learn and how that learning will be applied on-the-job. | YES/NO/Don't Know |
| | 8. Supervisors/bosses of learners meet with their direct reports to set performance goals for the learning intervention. | YES/NO/Don't Know |
| | 9. Supervisors/bosses of learners encourage and support learners as they participate in the learning intervention and attempt to apply new knowledge, skills, attitudes, and beliefs on-the-job. | YES/NO/Don't Know |

| FACTORS | QUESTIONS | RESPONSE |
|---|---|---|
| Application | 10. Learners have the opportunity within 48 hours to apply new knowledge, skills, attitudes, and beliefs to achieving business goals for themselves, their teams, and the organization. | YES/NO/Don't Know |
| | 11. Learners have the resources they need to apply their learning. | YES/NO/Don't Know |
| | 12. Application of newly developed competencies is valued by the organization. | YES/NO/Don't Know |
| Accountability | 13. Impact of learning on achieving business goals is measured. | YES/NO/Don't Know |
| | 14. Learners are recognized and rewarded for applying new learning to achieve business goals. | YES/NO/Don't Know |
| | 15. Performance data is used to improve learning interventions and enhance impact. | YES/NO/Don't Know |

Review your answers.
What are the implications of your answers for learning in your organization? Which of the 5As is strong in your organization and which are weak? What would you like to change? How are you going to do that?

Resources.

# 10

# Resources

## General

Broad, M.L. & Newstrom, J.W. Transfer of Training: Action-Packed Strategies to Ensure High Payoff from Training Investments, Reading, Mass: Addison-Wesley Publishing Company, 1992.

Gill, S.J. The 5 As of Performance Improvement, Customer Strategy Review (e-Newsletter), December 2006.

www.realtimeperformance.com/blog
www.theperformanceimprovementblog.com

## Alignment

Aligning learning to the needs of the organization, CIPD, February 2009: http://www.cipd.co.uk/subjects/lrnanddev/general/alignlearng.htm

Kaplan, R.S. & Norton, D.P. Strategy Maps: Converting Intangible Assets Into Tangible Outcomes, Boston: Harvard Business School Press, 2004.

Gill, S.J. Shifting Gears for High Performance, Training & Development, May, 1995.

Gill, S.J. Linking Training to Performance Goals, ASTD INFO-LINE, June 1996.

## Anticipation

Markovits, Michael & von Donop, Kristin, Collaborate for Growth: Deepening Involvement through Hope, Organization Development Journal, Volume 25: Number 4, Winter 2007

Weinstein, Rhona, Reaching Higher Power: The Power of Expectations in Schooling, Harvard University Press, 2004.

## Alliance

Brinkerhoff, R.O. & Gill, S.J. The Learning Alliance: Systems Thinking in Human Resource Development, San Francisco: Jossey-Bass Publishers, 1994.

Inspire, RealTime Performance. Web-based tool for creating high-quality individual learning plans. https://www.realtime360.com/inspire/

## Application

Implementing the Seven Principles: Technology as Lever, by Arthur W. Chickering and Stephen C. Ehrmann: http://www.tltgroup.org/programs/seven.html

Inspire, RealTime Performance. Web-based tool for creating high-quality individual learning plans. https://www.realtime360.com/inspire/

## Accountability

Brinkerhoff, R.O. Telling Training's Story: Evaluation Made Simple, Credible, and Effective, San Francisco: Barrett-Koehler Publishers, 2006.

Mooney, T. and Brinkerhoff, R.O. Courageous Training: Bold Actions for Business Results. San Francisco: Barrett-Koehler Publishers, 2008.

Are You Too Nice to Train, by Sarah Boehle, Training Magazine, August 2006
http://www.trainingmag.com/msg/content_display/training/e3iwtqVX4kKzJL%2BEcpyFJFrFA%3D%3D#

# About the Authors

## Stephen J. Gill

Stephen J. Gill is an independent consultant who, for the past 25 years, has been measuring the impact of learning interventions, such as training and coaching, and helping organizations improve the performance of individual employees and teams. He is a former university professor and a widely published author. Steve has an undergraduate degree from the University of Minnesota and M.A. and Ph.D. degrees from Northwestern University in counseling psychology. Steve lives in Ann Arbor, Michigan with his wife and dog. Steve writes the blog, http://www.theperformanceimprovementblog.com

# About the Authors, *continued*

## Sean P. Murray

Sean P. Murray is the founder and president of RealTime Performance, a company dedicated to elevating the quality of leadership globally. Founded in 1999, RealTime Performance provides leadership training, consulting and web-based tools to help clients accelerate the development of leaders. RealTime Performance has consulted to a number of Fortune 500 companies including Johnson & Johnson, FedEx, Nordstrom, Lockheed Martin, PepsiCo and Starbucks. Sean has an undergraduate degree from the University of Puget Sound and a Master of Business Administration from the University of Oregon. Sean lives in Seattle with his wife and two children. Sean writes the RealTime Leadership blog at http://www.realtimeperformance.com/blog/.

Notes

Notes

If you would like help applying the
5As Framework at your organization,
or implementing the 5As Framework audit,
please contact RealTime Performance:

RealTime Performance
603 Stewart Street, Suite 500
Seattle, WA 98101
Tel: (206) 749-9000
www.realtimeperformance.com

# Index.

# Index



## A



## B



## C

## R



## S



## T



## V



## W

GETTING MORE FROM YOUR INVESTMENT IN TRAINING
5 A's